Speedway

Tony Norman

FULL FLIGHT

Titles in Full Flight

Badger Publishing Limited
26 Wedgwood Way, Pin Green Industrial Estate, Stevenage,
Hertfordshire SG1 4QF
Telephone: 01438 356907. Fax: 01438 747015.
www.badger-publishing.co.uk   enquiries@badger-publishing.co.uk

Speedway ISBN 1 85880 927 4

Series Editor: Jonny Zucker.
Publisher: David Jamieson.
Editor: Paul Martin.
Cover design: Jain Birchenough.
Cover photographs: Alan Whale.

Photographs © Tony Norman (pp. 1, 7, 16, 22, 26, 29), © Alan Whale
(pp. 4, 11, 13, 14, 20, 31), © John Gaisford (pp. 8, 18, 20 - below).

Speedway

Tony Norman

Contents

Badger Publishing

1: Red Hot Racers

The speedway stadium is packed. The fans look tense, as they wait to see their heroes.

Suddenly, four top riders burst out onto the track and the crowd goes wild.

The cheers almost drown out the roar of the motor bikes, as they cruise to the starting line.

The speedway stars wear leather racing suits and coloured helmets. They look cool, like comic book heroes.

They line their bikes up at the starting gate and rev their engines to full power. It's time to focus hard on the race head.

Then the starting gate whips up into the air. The bikes rush forward and speed into the first corner. They are just centimetres apart, as they slide round the bend.

The racers have just one thing on their minds and that's winning.

Welcome to UK speedway, the home of the red hot racers!

2. The Elite League

Speedway stars from all round the world race in the UK's Elite League.

British riders can test their skills against the best.

Each team has seven riders and the season lasts from spring to autumn.

There are 15 races at every meeting. Each race lasts four laps of the track.

Two riders from each team take part.

Place	Points
Winner	3
Second	2
Third	1

Only the first three riders get points for their team. The team with the most points after 15 races wins the match.

At the end of the season, the top five teams in the league go into a play-off series. The teams race each other. The top team become the new champions.

There are other speedway leagues in the UK, where young riders can learn their skills. Most dream of racing in the Elite League some day. It's the best in the world!

3. The Track

Oxford Stadium

Speedway tracks are oval. At the top and bottom of the track, there are bends. The sides are straight.

Most tracks are about 400 metres long. Top riders can do a lap in 15 seconds.

Elite League races last four laps. Riders can hit speeds of 70-80 mph. Races last about a minute.

Speedway tracks are not hard and smooth, like a road. They are made of shale. This is a loose mix of small stones and gravel. The riders slide their bikes round the bends at high speed.

There is a safety net all round the track, in case a bike crashes.

Between races, the riders wait in the pits. This is a safe area, away from the track, where all the bikes are kept.

Every track has a starting gate. When the speedway racers roar into action, all eyes are on the track!

4. The Race

What's it like to race in the Elite League? Here's how top riders see the action...

The speedway racers ride up to the starting gate.

Four boxes are marked out on the track, behind the start line. One for each rider. Riders from the same team never start side by side.

A green light on the starting gate tells the riders there are five seconds to go. The race starts and the bikes go from zero to 60 mph - in two seconds!

They zoom into the first bend. The
bikes have no brakes. The riders
control their speed by the way they
slide round the loose track. Their bikes
are light and easy to handle.

The bikes race round the bend and out
into the first straight. The rider in front
knows he has the best chance of
winning the race. There are no bikes in
front of him; he can really go for it.

Another bonus is he can see where he's going. Dirt from the front bike flies up into the faces of the riders behind. They have to keep their goggles clean. This takes time and, in a top race, every second counts.

Tactics for the rest of the race are simple.

The race leader tries to block out the other riders. He must make sure they have no room to pass. The chasing bikes buzz around like wasps, waiting for a mistake. Bikes can pass on the inside or outside of the track.

Sometimes riders overtake on the straight, when their bikes are roaring at full power. But most races are won and lost on the bends. That's where the skill of the best riders really shines through.

Speedway racers go for it... all the way to the finish line.

5. Top Riders

Gary Havelock with his mechanics

Gary Havelock is captain of Poole Pirates, a top Elite League team.

"Speedway racers must be brave," says Gary. "But you should never take chances out on the track. That can mean danger for you and the other riders. Races should be won on skill alone."

Tony Rickardsson has been world champion. What makes a winner?

"Top riders are the same in lots of ways. They all have fast bikes and talent," Tony says.

"So, at the start of every race, you must feel you are the one who can come out on top. If you believe it deep inside, you can go out and win the race."

As captain of Poole Pirates, Gary likes to see good team spirit.

"Elite League speedway is a team sport, on the track and in the pits. If you all work hard for each other, you can go far."

6. In The Pits

The pits are a safe area, off to the side of the track. Bikes are kept here between races.

"All the riders have two bikes, maybe more," says top mechanic Andy Cooper. "If one breaks down, you need another just in case.

"Speedway bikes are very light and have a four-stroke 500cc engine. They have no brakes and no gears. They can go from zero to 60 mph in 25 metres.

"Riders have their own mechanics to tune their bikes between races. When riders are late for the start of a race, they get a 'two minute warning'. If there's a job to be done on the bike in that time, it can make the mechanic sweat a bit. You have to know how to deal with the pressure."

Speedway fans love seeing the thrills on the track. And there's lots more drama behind-the-scenes too... in the pits!

7. Top Managers

Colin Meredith and Vanessa Purchase with the League Cup

Colin Meredith is the manager of Oxford Cheetahs, who have won the Elite League. He raced for the team in the 1970s and rode for England.

"Being an ex-rider helps you to be a good manager," Colin says.

"You know how riders think and feel. You've been there too."

During a match, managers work in the pits with their riders and mechanics.

Colin has to pick two riders from his team for each of the 15 races. He knows his tactics can win or lose the match. All managers feel the strain.

"When a match is close, managers have to think hard and act fast. That's when your heart beats faster. It's very exciting.

"If we're losing a match but then come through to win, it's the best feeling in the world. Those are the times you never forget."

8. On The Road

Speedway Racers travel in style!

When a team races away from home, the days start early and end late.

 Vanessa Purchase is the promoter of Oxford Cheetahs.

"We like our team to be at the track an hour early," says Vanessa. "That gives them time to focus on the meeting ahead.

"Our riders all travel in their own trucks with their own mechanics. The bikes go in the back. In the front there's usually somewhere to sleep, plus things like a TV, microwave and fridge.

"Our riders need good transport. They're on the road so much during the season."

Many riders race in Europe too. They drive up to 50,00 miles a year. All that travel may sound cool, but there's no time for sight-seeing.

If you want to be a speedway racer, you'd better get ready for life on the road.

It's tough!

9. Speedway on TV

For TV fans, Tony Millard is the voice of speedway on Sky Sports.

"I want viewers to feel close to the action," says Tony. "It's not good to talk too much. I let the pictures tell some of the story."

What does he like best about his job?

"You never know what's going to happen next. That's exciting. Speedway is full of speed and drama. It's a great sport, it really is.

"On live TV you must never stop talking, no matter what. Once, I started to lose my voice halfway through a match. I just about made it to the end of last race and that was it. I couldn't talk for a week!"

And his happiest memory?

"Doing the commentary when Eastbourne Eagles won the Elite League in 2000. I have been close to the club for many years, so that was very special."

10. Headline News

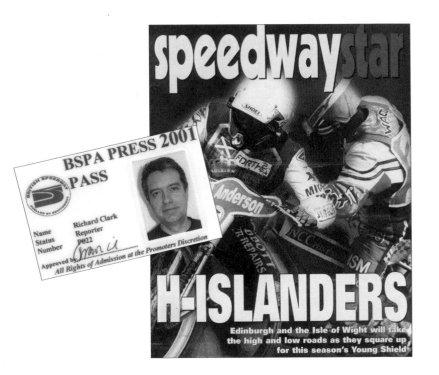

Richard Clark is the Editor of Speedway Star magazine. And that makes him one of the UK's top writers on the sport.

"I think the top racers are very brave people," says Richard.

"Let's face it, every time they go out to race they risk their lives. They don't like to talk about that, but it's true just the same." Richard has travelled the world to watch speedway.

"I once flew to Australia to cover a big tour. We got to Sydney and I was really keen to enjoy some top class racing. Then a storm hit the city and the match was washed out. It was a long way to go, just to watch the rain!"

But for Richard, rainy days are few and far between.

"I earn a living, writing about my favourite sport," he smiles. "Who could ask for more?"

11. Young Stars

Junior training session at the Eastbourne Eagles Track

The future is looking good for speedway. But how do the young stars of tomorrow learn to ride?

Speedway is dangerous. If you don't know what you're doing, you can get badly hurt.

So, it's best to take some lessons from a top coach. Many speedway clubs help young riders in this way.

Colin Ackroyd used to race for Eastbourne Eagles. Now he trains young riders on the club's youth track.

"Speedway is a great sport," says Colin, "but it's not a good idea to push too hard too soon. Lots of young riders are keen to get into racing right away. I can see why, but the truth is you need to know how to control your bike safely first. Then you can move on from there."

Some speedway schools have bikes you can hire. Some young riders have their own. Safety equipment must be worn:

- a helmet and goggles
- gloves
- leathers
- a back protector
- proper footwear.

You look good and feel safe.

"Youngsters should learn at their own pace," Colin explains. "It can take a while to feel good out on the track. When a rider is confident, that's the time to learn new skills."

Colin has worked with many young stars. In 2001, Edward Kennett signed for Eastbourne Eagles when he was 15 years old. That made him the club's youngest ever rider.

Edward had won the British under-15 speedway championship four times. Now there's James Walker. James won the title when he was only 10.

"They are both very good," says Colin. "The kids who train with us can't all be champions, but they can all have fun. That's important to me. I like to see lots of smiles from our young riders!"

12. Final Flag

It's nearly the end of the race. The riders finish their third lap.

A yellow and black flag waves. One lap to go. Who will be the winner?

The buzz in the stadium is fantastic!

In the pits, riders cheer their team-mates on. Managers and promoters are yelling too. Reporters scribble notes to catch the action. TV commentators bring the action alive for fans at home.

Somewhere in the roaring crowd, a young speedway rider dreams of being out in the bright lights. One day, in the future, he will be a hero too.

The bikes roar round the final bend.
The crowd save their biggest cheers for
last. The winner takes a lap of honour
and throws in some classic wheelies.

The final flag falls on our book about
speedway. Hope you've enjoyed the ride!

Index